Ḥajj & 'Umrah

Ḥajj & 'Umrah

A Practical and Spiritual Guide to the Journey

MUSTAFA UMAR

ḤAJJ & ʿUMRAH

First Edition

ISBN-13: 978-1517470067

ISBN-10: 1517470064

In the Name of God

The Most Kind and Merciful

Contents

Introduction	9
What is Ḥajj and ʿUmrah	13
Virtues of Ḥajj	17
Who Must Perform Ḥajj	22
Choosing a Type of Ḥajj	26
Mīqāt Boundaries	28
Entering the State of Iḥrām	32
Arriving in Makkah & Visiting the Mosque	43
Ṭawāf Qudūm/Taḥiyyah	46
Walking [*Saʿy*] between Ṣafā and Marwah	56
Release from Iḥrām	61
Day One—8th of Dhul Ḥijjah	63
Day Two—9th of Dhul Ḥijjah	65
Day Three—10th of Dhul Ḥijjah	69

Day Four—11th of Dhul Ḥijjah 75

Day Five—12th of Dhul Ḥijjah 76

Day Six [Optional]—13th of Dhul Ḥijjah 77

Mistakes and Penalties 79

What to do in Makkah 84

Visiting Madīnah 86

Appendix: The Standard Ḥajj Schedule 89

Appendix: Selected Supplications [*duʿāʾ*] and Remembrances [*dhikr*] 90

Appendix: The Funeral Prayer 93

Appendix: Differences of Opinion 94

Appendix: Avoiding Difficulties 98

References 100

Introduction

Every capable Muslim must perform Ḥajj at least once in their lifetime, as soon as they are reasonably able to do so. It is essential for a believer to not only learn the rules concerning this Pilgrimage but also to understand the purpose and spirit behind the motions. When the ultimate purpose of Ḥajj is achieved with sincerity, this spiritual journey rises from being a lifeless ritual of blind imitation to a source of forgiveness and transformation.

Muslims fortunate enough to undertake the journey to Makkah often struggle to understand what exactly they are supposed to do and they become confused during the journey. Oftentimes this occurs because they failed to properly educate themselves. Knowing exactly what to do and what to expect not only ensures that the Ḥajj is performed correctly but can also prevent other difficulties associated with the already challenging trip. Ḥajj is a once-in-a-lifetime opportunity and, thus, deserves proper preparation.

Sometimes, however, even after attending a seminar or reading a book, a person may have practical questions that go unanswered, which can result in mistakes or just result in frustration. I personally experienced some anxiety during my first journey of Ḥajj because, even after having attended a seminar and reading through several books, it was clear that I had not prepared enough. I firmly believe that a large part of the problem lies in the weaknesses of the teaching methods present in many seminars and books dealing with the subject.

One book should be sufficient for the average educated Muslim to learn most of what they need to know. Therefore, I believe there remains an urgent need for a simple and concise, but comprehensive, guide which teaches all the basics of Ḥajj and ʿUmrah. The present book has been designed for people who have never performed either Ḥajj or ʿUmrah before or those who did not learn correctly or thoroughly.

This work aims to resolve such deficiencies by using an 'assume-nothing and teach-everything' methodology. Such a technique assumes that the reader has little background knowledge of Islām and thus everything will be explained in detail without assuming that the person is familiar with certain terms, places, and concepts. A step-by-step presentation of what a person should do will be included along with maps and photos to aid descriptions. The book will aim to cover the legal aspects of Ḥajj which are most likely to occur, the rational and spiritual dimensions behind each act, and the historical origins of places and rituals.

The truth is that I have written this book for myself to remind me of all the things I need to know for my upcoming trip. I plan on keeping this work with me so I know what to do, why I am doing it, and the answers to most questions that may arise in my mind while I am in the midst of my journey.

HOW TO USE THIS BOOK

I recommend that you read through the entire book at least once prior to departure. Afterwards, during the journey, read each section in its entirety right before you are about to perform that act so you know exactly what will come next and will be prepared for anything you specifically need to be careful of.

Try to memorize some of the supplications [see the appendix on 'Selected Supplications'] and words that are to be said during Ḥajj so you don't have to hold a book in your hand. If this is difficult, at least keep the book handy with you when performing those steps.

Remember that the requirements in any given section are 'all-inclusive'. This means that if a commonly occurring scenario has not been explicitly mentioned, then it is not a requirement. Likewise, nothing is recommended unless it has specifically been mentioned. For example, if you see some people washing the stones that they will use to throw at the stone pillars but you do not find this act mentioned in this book, then know that the act of washing the pebbles was omitted from this book on purpose, since it is neither a requirement nor a recommendation. The principle to keep in mind is that in Islām, everything is lawful unless specifically prohibited and nothing is recommended [as a religious act of worship] unless explicitly specified.

What is Ḥajj and 'Umrah

Ḥajj is a religious journey to the city of Makkah and some other nearby regions. It commemorates the spirit of righteousness embodied by Prophet Ibrāhīm [Abraham] and his family. Ḥajj occurs only once a year from the 8th-12th in the lunar month of Dhul Ḥijjah. It is attended by about four to five million Muslims and is the largest annual gathering of people in the world.

'Umrah is a shortened version of Ḥajj which can take place at any time of the year in Makkah and only takes about an hour or two to complete. It is highly recommended to perform it at least once in a lifetime, even if you are unable to perform Ḥajj. Those who go for Ḥajj usually perform an 'Umrah as well during the same journey.

MAKKAH

Makkah is an ancient city in Western Arabia which was founded by Hājar [Hagar], the wife of Prophet Ibrāhīm. It is a narrow valley about 900 feet above sea level and 50 miles from the Red Sea. Prophet Ibrāhīm was instructed by Allāh to leave his wife Ḥājar and son Ismā'īl [Ishamel] in this barren valley as a test to see whether he and his wife are willing to overlook the principle of causality and put their trust in Allāh. They both passed their tests with flying colors and Allāh made the region of Makkah a special place.

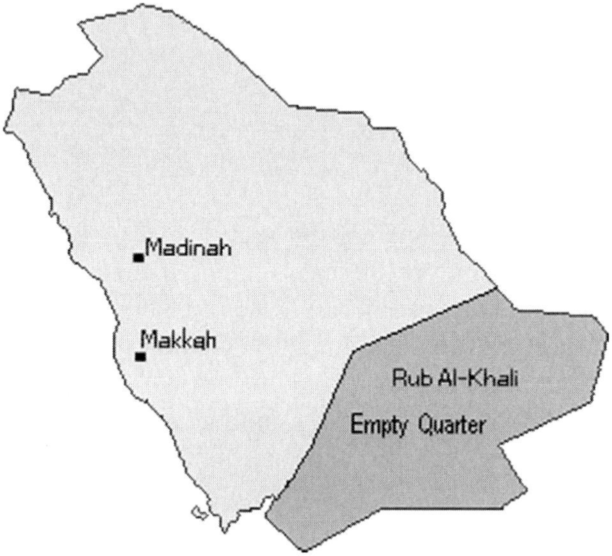

Map of Arabia

Ibrāhīm and his son built the Kaʿbah, which was the first building dedicated entirely to the worship of one God alone.[1] He instituted the Ḥajj Pilgrimage, where people have been visiting the once-empty valley for thousands of years.[2] Makkah now has a population of two million people [2012] and the word "Mecca" in English is used to refer to any place that attracts a lot of people. The city has been mentioned several times in the Qur'ān and is known as Umm al-Qurā [the mother of all settlements] because of

1 See Qur'ān 2:127-128, 3:96-97, 22:27-30

2 See Qur'ān 22:28

the prominent position it occupies in Arabia. The region has also been mentioned in the Bible as the wilderness of Parān in Genesis 21:21, although some Jewish and Christian scholars insist on giving another meaning to that verse.

The Kaʿbah c. 1850 C.E.

The Kaʿbah c. 2015 C.E.

Makkah's religious merit lies primarily in the fact that it contains the Kaʿbah, which all Muslims around the world face during prayer. However, the city also has immense historical value because the Prophet Muhammad lived there for most of his life and it was the place of the first thirteen years of the revelation of the Qur'ān.

Virtues of Ḥajj

ESCHATOLOGICAL DIMENSIONS

Ḥajj has the potential of being one of the most rewarding acts of worship you can ever perform. The Prophet said, "Whoever performs Ḥajj [sincerely] for Allāh and avoids obscenity and sins will return [from the journey] like the day his mother gave him birth [i.e. with no sins]."[3] It is important to remember that the aforementioned benefits are conditional upon the Ḥajj being fulfilled properly. Do not assume that you will automatically receive a get-out-of-hell-free ticket just by performing the motions of Ḥajj. It is also important to keep in mind the warning of the Prophet, "It might be that a person who fasts gains nothing from it except hunger and a person who prays gains nothing from it except fatigue."[4] The principle that insincere or incorrect acts of worship result in reduced rewards can also apply to Ḥajj.

3 Bukhārī #1521, 2:133. Also see Qur'ān 2:197.

4 Ibn Mājah #1690, 1:539, graded ḥasan ṣaḥīḥ [authentic] by Shaykh Albānī

SOCIAL DIMENSIONS

Ḥajj has far reaching social dimensions as well. The American revolutionary Malcolm X described his experience in these words:

> *There were tens of thousands of pilgrims, from all over the world. They were of all colors, from blue-eyed blondes to black-skinned Africans. But we were all participating in the same ritual, displaying a spirit of unity and brotherhood that my experiences in America had led me to believe never could exist between the white and the non-white. America needs to understand Islām, because this is the one religion that erases from its society the race problem. You may be shocked by these words coming from me. But on this pilgrimage, what I have seen, and experienced, has forced me to rearrange much of my thought patterns previously held.*[5]

PREPARING MENTALLY & SPIRITUALLY

It is important for you to prepare for the journey both mentally and spiritually. Here are some tips:

- Rectify your intention: The ultimate purpose of performing Ḥajj is to worship Allāh and follow what He instructed. It is essential to remove any worldly intentions that interfere with that ultimate purpose. Some people think of Ḥajj primarily as a vacation, others go to Makkah mainly to do business, and yet others are lured into the trap of excessive shopping. There is no harm in conducting business or even shopping during

---

5 Malcolm X with the assistance of Alex Haley, The Autobiography of Malcolm X, 371.

Ḥajj, but this should never be the primary goal or occupation during this spiritual journey.

- Make preparations for death: In the past, Ḥajj was a more dangerous journey than it is today. Therefore, people would make sure to pay off their debts and write their will before leaving, although these things should be taken care of even if one is not going for Ḥajj.
- Be conscious of Allāh: Remember that Allāh is watching you throughout your journey and knows what is truly in your heart. Although He is always aware, you should try to be on your best behavior during the Ḥajj, both internally and externally.
- Exercise patience: Ḥajj is full of challenges that can potentially be nerve-wrecking. In the past people would travel through the rough desert for weeks and experience the extreme temperatures of Makkah during their Ḥajj. Now, with the advent of high-speed transportation and the conveniences of air conditioning, such difficulties have been removed almost entirely. However, these difficulties have been substituted with other challenges such as overcrowding and the negative effects of globalization. It is highly likely that you will see and experience things that bother you, or are outright unjust (to either yourself or another person). Be prepared and do not allow these experiences to distract you from your ultimate goal. If something is within your immediate ability to correct, then go ahead. Otherwise, realize and accept the fact that you cannot 'fix' the problems you see in the worldwide Muslim community during your Ḥajj journey. Be prepared to remain calm in any event. You may be pushed or shoved, even in front of the Kaʿbah. You might

have your money stolen while inside the mosque. The airport might lose your luggage or passport. The important thing to remember is that if you are wronged, stay calm. You might be able to deal with the injustice immediately or you may have to wait until the Ḥajj is over. By losing your cool, you can potentially lose your Ḥajj, and it is not worth it.[6]

- Be merciful: Because it is easy to harm someone during Ḥajj due to the massive crowds of people, you should be extra careful. Avoid pushing or shoving, even if it means you have to wait for a long time. Ḥajj is not the time to insist on justice but rather to focus on mercy, the same way you want Allāh's mercy to supersede His justice when dealing with you. Also, go out of your way to help other people, whether it is making extra space for them, helping them with their luggage, or serving people food.
- Be clean: With the millions of people packed into Makkah at the same time, it is important to be extra careful about cleanliness when using bathrooms and to make sure you throw all garbage away in its proper place. If anyone is harmed by your waste you will be held responsible in front of Allāh.
- Keep good company: It is easy to get distracted during Ḥajj and end up wasting time in excessive socialization. Make sure to avoid that by staying in the company of people who really want to focus on worshipping Allāh during their Ḥajj. It is important to be polite but firm when demanding that people leave you alone. Setting a serious tone from the beginning of the journey will

6 See Qur'ān 2:197

prevent others from assuming that you are the type of person they can 'kill time' with when they are bored.

- Prepare to change your life: Ḥajj is about dedicating yourself to Allāh. It is not about being a good Muslim for a few days and then going back to your old bad habits. After Ḥajj, a person should prepare to start a new life by giving up all doubtful and sinful practices they used to partake in. It is good practice to redress any wrongs you have committed towards others before leaving and to be prepared to make a vow to Allāh that you will do your utmost to be the best Muslim you can be after you return.

Who Must Perform Ḥajj

Ḥajj is an obligation[7] at least once in a lifetime for Muslims who are able to go. It is one of the five pillars upon which Islām stands and should never be neglected or delayed. As soon as you are able, you must immediately go that year.

Only the following Muslims are exempted from performing Ḥajj:

- Children: A person is only held responsible for their actions in the sight of Allāh after he has attained maturity and their intellect has developed.[8] This occurs when a child reaches puberty. A boy is considered to be a mature adult when he has his first wet dream [or equivalent]. A girl is considered to be mature when she either has her first wet dream [or equivalent] or begins her menstrual period. If neither of these

7 See Qur'ān 3:97

8 The exact time when this happens is only known to Allāh. However, we must approximate when this occurs for legal reasons to distinguish between a child and an adult, hence the following criteria specified in Islamic law.

occurs by the age of fifteen[9] they are considered to be mature at that age.

- ✧ Young children who cannot fully understand what they are doing may still perform Ḥajj. Their parents will get the reward for allowing them to experience this Islāmic activity. Children old enough to understand what they are doing will benefit from its performance. They should try to do Ḥajj as best as they can, but it will not lift the obligation from them. Therefore, when they reach the age of maturity, they will have to perform it again as soon as they are able.

- Mentally handicapped: People who are afflicted with an illness or defect that impairs their intellect are not considered responsible adults. They are treated like children in that they are not held accountable for their actions in this world or the next. However, they may still perform Ḥajj and go through the motions, just like children do.

- Financially unable: Someone who is unable to afford the expenses of traveling to Makkah and back, paying for the stay there, and having their family taken care of while they are gone, is not required to perform Ḥajj. Ḥajj can be quite costly nowadays. A person should try to find the most economical travel package they can and go if they can afford it.
  - ✧ It is important to note that a person should not borrow money in order to perform the Ḥajj. Also, paying off immediate debts takes priority over going for Ḥajj, since that money actually belongs to someone else.

9 This is calculated in lunar years according to Islamic law.

- Physically unable: A person who is physically unable to undertake the journey due to severe discomfort or other reasons is exempted from performing Ḥajj. However, there are many facilities for disabled people, such as wheelchairs and escorts for those who can afford them, which would keep the obligation intact for these people.
- Relative danger of the journey: If there is a highly probable likelihood of danger when traveling to Ḥajj then a person is exempted. In the past, people faced desert bandits or sea pirates when traveling long distances and sometimes had to go in armed groups to protect themselves.
    - ✧ It is a requirement for women to have a male relative [maḥram], such as her brother or uncle, accompany her on the Ḥajj to ensure her safety. However, if she is unable to have a family escort and there is probable certainty that her journey will be relatively safe, this requirement is overlooked. Nonetheless, the current government of Saudi Arabia has placed specific visa restrictions concerning women in accordance with their understanding of Islāmic Law on this issue, so check with your local embassy.

QUESTIONS

- If I have borrowed money from a bank to purchase a house do I have to go for Ḥajj since I would not have any money left if I paid it off?

Having a loan on your house has no impact on your ability to go for Ḥajj since the agreement with the bank is to make monthly payments rather than to pay off the loan immediately. Therefore, your entire housing debt is not 'currently due', rather, only your monthly payment is, and that can be subtracted from your assets when determining whether or not you can afford Ḥajj.

Choosing a Type of Ḥajj

There are three ways to perform Ḥajj, and any of them is fine, since the Prophet said, "It is fine to perform Ḥajj and ʿUmrah together, Ḥajj [alone], or ʿUmrah [followed by Ḥajj]."[10]

A person must pick one of three methods to follow:

- Merging ʿUmrah into Ḥajj as two separate acts [tamattuʿ]: This form of Ḥajj is easier if you arrive in Makkah early because it lifts some of the restrictions on you, and allows you to wear normal clothes between the time of your initial arrival and the start of Ḥajj on the 8th of Dhul Ḥijjah. It is called 'tamattuʿ', which means enjoyment, because it makes your life a little easier. Most people today choose this type of Ḥajj either because it is easier or because some scholars believe it is the recommended method.
- Combining ʿUmrah and Ḥajj together as one act [qirān]: 'Qirān' means to combine two things into one. This type of Ḥajj requires a person to remain in special clothing and observe certain restrictions for a longer

10 See Bukhārī & Muslim

period of time. If someone arrives in Makkah very close to the starting date of Ḥajj, then it is not that difficult to perform this type.

- Ḥajj only [ifrād]: 'Ifrād' means to single something out. In this case, no ʿUmrah is performed as a part of the Ḥajj. Most people who perform this type of Ḥajj are those who live in Makkah because they have ample opportunity to perform ʿUmrah throughout the year.

QUESTIONS

- Which type of Ḥajj is better?

Some scholars have said that qirān is better because it is more difficult. Others believe that tamattuʿ is better because the Prophet advised some of his Companions to change their Ḥajj to this form. There are even scholars who argue that ifrād is superior. It is best to follow your group leader. Also note that the Ḥajj travel package you have chosen and the specific itinerary may restrict the types of Ḥajj you are able perform.

Mīqāt Boundaries

BACKGROUND

People used to come from all directions to visit Makkah. Since the Ḥajj actually begins [by wearing certain clothing] prior to entering the city, the

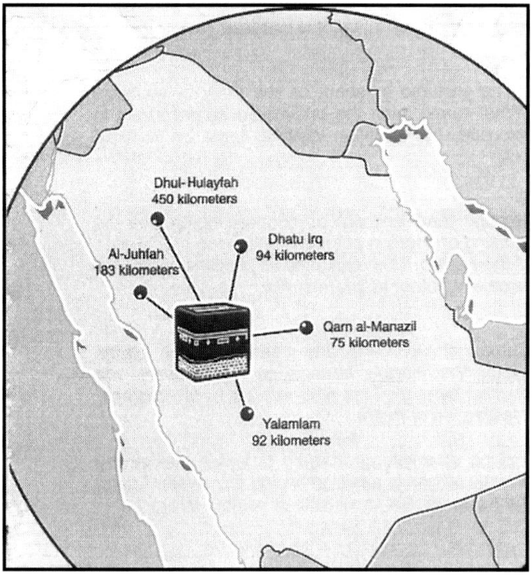

Locations of Mīqāt Boundaries

Prophet fixed certain starting points. These were known locations where people would stop and rest on their way to Makkah from different parts of the world.

There are five specified locations [known as 'mīqāt'] where people from certain regions would normally pass through:

LOCATION	PEOPLE COMING FROM THE DIRECTION OF
Juḥfah	*Syria*
Dhul Ḥulayfah	*Madīnah*
Dhātu ʿIrq	*Iraq*
Qarn Al-Manāzil	*Najd*
Yalamlam	*Yemen*

Nowadays, a pentagon is formed from these five points and anyone crossing into this region, with the intention to visit Makkah, must begin their Ḥajj or ʿUmrah from this location. Some of these locations have been renamed, but knowledgeable people will recognize the original names.

If you live within these boundaries, even in Makkah, you will begin Ḥajj from your current location. However, the people living in Makkah must travel outside the boundaries of the city if they want to perform ʿUmrah, since it is a regularly occurring event, unlike Ḥajj which only happens once a year.

It is important to pay close attention to these locations, especially when traveling by plane. If you cross the mīqāt boundary without beginning Ḥajj, you will need to sacrifice an animal as a penalty for that mistake. Making such a mistake out of carelessness or neglect would also be considered a sin.

Dhul Ḥulayfah Mosque

QUESTIONS

- If I want to do some business in Jeddah [which is inside the mīqāt boundaries], do I have to begin a Ḥajj or ʿUmrah?

  No, since you do not have the intention to go to Makkah in the first place.

- If I plan to arrive in Jeddah [which is inside the mīqāt boundary] and stay there a while to visit some friends, then travel to Makkah after that, where do I begin my Ḥajj from?

  You will begin your Ḥajj or ʿUmrah from Jeddah, just like the people who live there. This is because the initial intention of your first journey was to visit Jeddah and not Makkah. It might be that you remain in Jeddah for a longer period than you had anticipated. Once you make the intention to leave

Jeddah for Makkah, you will be in the same state as a resident of Jeddah.

- If I merge ʿUmrah into Ḥajj [tamattuʿ] by going to Makkah and performing ʿUmrah, then leave for Madīnah, do I have to perform another ʿUmrah from Dhul Ḥulayfah upon my return to Makkah for Ḥajj?

  No, because the purpose of merging ʿUmrah into Ḥajj [tamattuʿ] is to take a break from clothing restrictions until the days of Ḥajj begin on the 8th of Dhul Ḥijjah.

Entering the State of Iḥrām

BACKGROUND

Iḥrām is the state in which a person must be in order to perform Ḥajj or ʿUmrah. It is similar to initiating prayer by raising your hands near your ears and saying 'Allāhu Akbar' ['God is the greatest']. Once you are in prayer you must avoid certain things that would invalidate it, such as laughing or turning around. Likewise, for iḥrām, you must wear certain clothing and avoid certain things that would violate it, such as cutting your hair or nails.

WEAR IḤRĀM CLOTHING

There is special clothing to wear when you are in the state of iḥrām to signify simplicity and humility before Allāh. Since this clothing can be difficult to wear because people are not used to it, it is fine to put it on at the most convenient place, even if that is several hours before reaching the mīqāt boundaries.

Prepare to Enter Iḥrām

Before assuming iḥrām, it is recommended to:

- clip your nails
- shave/trim your underarm and pubic hair
- [men] trim your moustache
- take a bath [or perform wuḍū' if bathing is inconvenient]
- apply perfume [or deodorant] on your body

Immediately before wearing iḥrām clothing it is recommended to pray two units first and recite sūrah al-kāfirūn [109] in the first unit and sūrah al-ikhlāṣ [112] in the second. If you happen to have just performed a prayer, like ẓuhr or maghrib, there is no need to pray again before wearing iḥrām clothing.

Clothing Requirements

FOR MEN

- Wear two 'unstitched' sheets or towels, one for the lower body to cover the private parts and the other for the upper body to protect you from the weather.
  - ✧ 'Unstitched' clothing is that which is not sewn together in order to wrap around limbs of the body the way that shirts or pants are stitched together for that purpose.
  - ✧ It is recommended that these garments be white in color.
- Wear sandals or slippers that do not cover most of your upper foot. Make sure that your ankles, your back heel, and most of the surface of your upper foot are exposed.

- Do not cover your face, hands, or head with anything resembling clothing.

FOR WOMEN

- Women have different dress requirements because unstitched garments are not as conducive to female modesty. Therefore, they are allowed to wear any type and color of modest dress, even if it is stitched. Wearing socks and shoes are fine for women as well.
- The only dress requirement for women is that they are not allowed to cover their face or hands.

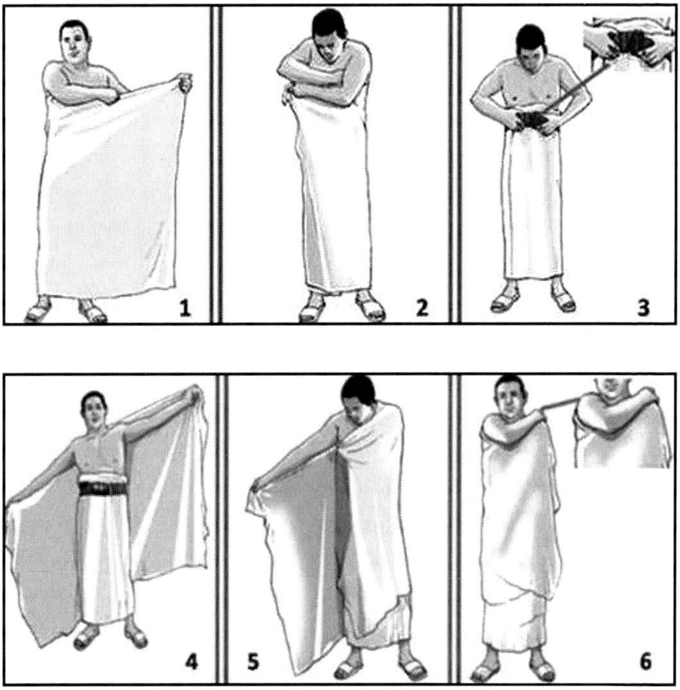

How to Wear Iḥrām Clothing

Tips

Wear your iḥrām clothing in an airport rather than on the airplane since it is usually very cramped on the plane.

When wearing the lower iḥrām garment, make sure you have wrapped it in a way that there is enough space for mobility so you can spread your legs when needed.

Apply anti-chaffing cream [if needed] between your inner thighs to prevent chaffing of the skin. This condition can make walking quite painful, so prevent it before it happens.

Questions

- Can I enter into iḥrām during my menstrual period or lochia [postpartum discharge]?

  Yes. Women are not allowed to pray, fast, or walk around the Kaʿbah when they are in this state, but are still able to perform all the other parts of the Ḥajj. There is no need to worry since you are not missing out on any requirements of Ḥajj. You might opt to take medicine that bypasses your period for one month. This is relatively safe and any spotting you see during that time is abnormal blood, not menstrual blood.

- Should I take a bath [or perform wuḍū'] when entering into iḥrām even during my during my menstrual period or lochia [postpartum discharge]?

  Yes, it is still recommended to do so since it is symbolic and not for the purpose of prayer.

- Is it allowed to wear a belt, fanny pack, or backpack while in iḥrām clothing, even though they wrap around the body?

  Yes, it is allowed because they are considered to be accessories and not actual clothing, therefore there is no harm even if they wrap around part of the body. The same is the case with sandals where they must wrap around part of the foot in order to stay on.

- Is it allowed to wrap a jacket around your body while in iḥrām?

  As long as a person does not put his arms into the sleeves of the jacket it would be considered 'carrying' the jacket as an accessory and not 'wearing' it, therefore it would be allowed.

- Does wearing sunglasses count as covering the face during iḥrām?

  No, since the glasses are mainly supported on the bridge of the nose and do not actually touch the face for the most part. Also, glasses are somewhat transparent and therefore do not resemble a face covering.

- Does wearing a surgical face mask to protect against germs count as covering the face during iḥrām?

  Yes, but since it covers only a small portion of the face, charity must be given as a penalty [see section on 'Mistakes and Penalties'].

- Is it allowed to use a safety pin to keep my iḥrām garments from constantly falling down?

  Yes, this is allowed because it does not strongly resemble sewing the garments together. The purpose behind wearing these garments is not so that they constantly keep falling off, therefore a pin would not violate the underlying purpose of the garments.

- If I use a sleeping bag and zip it closed, is that like wearing stitched clothing in iḥrām?

  No, because a sleeping bag resembles a blanket more than it does clothing, and it is fine to wrap a blanket around your body.

- Is it allowed to take shelter under a tree or tent, or use an umbrella?

  Yes, because what is forbidden is to wear something over the head, but in this case nothing is being worn since it is not physically touching or wrapping around.

- Is it allowed to cover the head or face with a blanket when sleeping?

  It is only allowed as long as it does not touch a significant portion of your face or head directly.

INTENTION FOR IḤRĀM

Once you have prayed and worn the proper clothing, you are still not considered to be in the state of iḥrām until you make the intention to begin Ḥajj or ʿUmrah.

It is recommended to say the intention out loud in any words like: "Allāh, I intend to perform Hajj, make it easy for me and accept it from me."

Once this is done, you are now in the state of iḥrām. It is important to enter iḥrām prior to crossing the mīqāt boundary line, therefore, if you are afraid you might be sleeping or will forget to make the intention, do it earlier. However, don't make the intention too early in case your departure time is delayed. Once you are in the state of iḥrām, you cannot simply abandon it until you complete your Ḥajj or ʿUmrah, otherwise it would be a sin [without an excuse].

Questions

- If I put on the iḥrām garments early, am I in the state of iḥrām?

  No. Putting on the iḥrām garments does not put you in the state of iḥrām. Completing the intention after putting on the garments puts you in the state of iḥrām.

- Can the intention for iḥrām be made prior to reaching the mīqāt boundary?

  Yes, and it may even be recommended, especially if you are afraid that you might forget, or that you might sleep while crossing the boundary.

- If I forgot to say the intention out loud, will I be considered to be in the state of iḥrām?

  If you made the intention in your heart to enter iḥrām but did not say it out loud, then yes it will count. However, if you were planning on making the intention but never actually did so, then it will not count.

THE RESPONSE SLOGAN [*Talbiyah*]

After making the intention, say the Response Slogan [known as 'talbiyah'] out loud:

لَبَّيْكَ اللَّهُمَّ لَبَّيْكَ
لَبَّيْكَ لَا شَرِيكَ لَك لَبَّيْكَ
إِنَّ الْحَمْدَ وَالنِّعْمَةَ لَك وَالْمُلْكَ
لَا شَرِيكَ لَك

labbayk allāhumma labbayk
labbayka la sharīka laka labbayk
innal-ḥamda, wan-niʿmata, laka wal-mulk
lā sharīka lak

I am here [at your service], Allāh, I am here.
I am here, you have no partner, I am here
All praise and blessings are Yours, as well as the dominion.
You have no partner.

While in the state of iḥrām for the next few days, it is recommended to continue reciting this slogan aloud every now and then. It is especially recommended to recite it during changes in your circumstances. For example, when day turns to night, you transition from sitting to standing, you enter or leave a place, you meet people or leave their company, etc. then say it out loud either once or thrice. Try not to say it so loud that it disturbs other people who may be praying, reading, sleeping, etc.

Questions

- Are women allowed to recite the Response Slogan [talbiyah] out loud?

  Yes, it is fine for women to also say it out loud unless there is some legitimate fear that their feminine voice might be immodest, in which case they should lower their voice slightly.

PROHIBITIONS IN IḤRĀM

While you are in the state of iḥrām, you must observe the following prohibitions to the best of your ability:

- Not wearing certain clothing
  - ✧ [men] No covering the head with a cap, scarf, or anything that touches these parts
  - ✧ No covering the face with anything that touches it
  - ✧ [men] No covering the feet with socks or shoes
- Not trimming or shaving any hair on the head or body
  - ✧ Bathing, washing the head, itching the body, combing the hair, and the like is fine even if some hair accidentally falls out, since that is not akin to cutting
- Not clipping the nails
- Not applying perfume on either the clothes or body
  - ✧ Any scent that was applied to the body prior to assuming iḥrām is fine and does not need to be wiped off.
  - ✧ Using anything that resembles the purpose of perfume like deodorant, scented body lotion, scented hand sanitizer, etc. is not permissible to use.
  - ✧ Using unscented or very lightly scented versions of soap, lotion, sunblock, deodorant or shampoo is fine if it will not leave a fragrance after using it.
- Not being intimate or kissing with desire
  - ✧ It is fine to touch your spouse without any desire of intimacy

- Not having sexual intercourse
  - ✧ Violating this rule could potentially invalidate your entire Ḥajj, so be extra careful.
- Not hunting animals or helping anyone to hunt
  - ✧ Killing insects such as flies, mosquitos, and ants is not considered hunting, especially when they are being an annoyance
  - ✧ Killing harmful animals such as mice, snakes, and scorpions is allowed for safety reasons and does not fall under the category of hunting.
- Not proposing or getting married

It is important to be extra careful not to commit any sins while in iḥrām, such as arguing, using foul language, etc.

If you need to violate one of the rules of iḥrām due to either a medical reason or severe discomfort, such as wearing a foot brace or shoes due to an injury, you may do so. There is no need for you to suffer severe discomfort. Instead, go ahead and violate that one specific part of iḥrām that is afflicting you and it will not be considered sinful since you have an excuse. However, you must pay a penalty to make up for violating the rules of iḥrām [see the section on 'Mistakes and Penalties'].

QUESTIONS

- What if the iḥrām clothing gets soiled with urine or blood?

  The same rules apply as for normal clothing in that the impurity must be removed prior to performing prayer.

- Can I wash my iḥrām clothing with soap?

Yes, as long as the soap is not heavily scented such that it leaves a fragrance after washing.

- If I have an injury on my head and need to shave off some hair, what should I do?

  This is considered to be a medical reason which would result in severe discomfort if not performed. Do what is needed and there will be no sin, but you must offer a penalty.

- If I accidentally violate the state of iḥrām by covering my head, putting on perfume, or trimming my nails, what should I do?

  First, you should immediately rectify the situation if possible, by uncovering your head or wiping off the perfume. Then, see the section on 'Mistakes and Penalties' to determine what must be done.

- Does smoking a cigarette violate the state of iḥrām?

  Technically, no, but smoking is prohibited in Islām so it should be avoided at all times, especially when in the special spiritual state of iḥrām. Likewise, lying and stealing are prohibited in Islām but will not technically violate the state of iḥrām, so be careful not to neglect the underlying purpose of Ḥajj by disobeying Allāh's guidance.

Arriving in Makkah & Visiting the Mosque

BACKGROUND

The immediate area surrounding the Kaʿbah where people pray is considered a mosque and now has a building surrounding it. The Kaʿbah is in the center of this

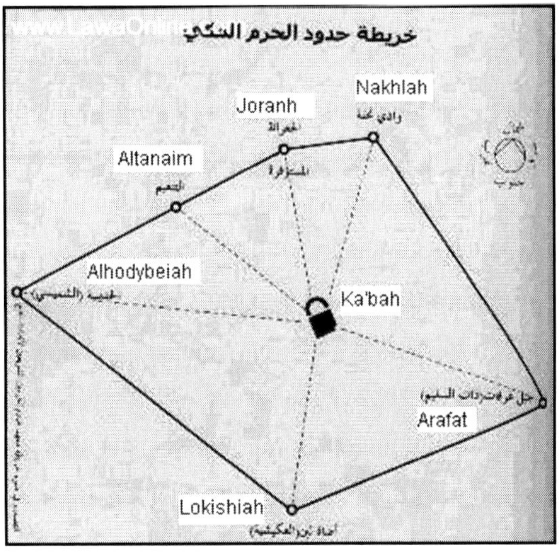

The Boundaries of Makkah

mosque in an open area. This entire area is known as the Sacred Mosque [al-Masjid al-Ḥarām] due to its special status.

The Kaʿbah c. 1907 C.E.

The Kaʿbah c. 2010 C.E.

VISITING THE SACRED MOSQUE

It is recommended to take a bath before entering Makkah, out of respect for the city, but due to high speed travel this bath can be performed from your last convenient point of departure. It is also recommended to go straight to the mosque, but nowadays you may have to take care of your belongings first and check in to your residence, unless someone else is handling that for you.

QUESTIONS

- Can menstruating women enter the Sacred Mosque [al-Masjid al-Ḥarām]?

  This mosque is no different than other mosques in that women must not enter while they are in a state of menstruation or lochia.

- Is it true that supplications are accepted when you first see the Kaʿbah?

  No, there is no strong evidence for that.

- Is there a special supplication to be made when looking at the Kaʿbah?

  Any supplication can be made and there is nothing that is recommended in particular.

Ṭawāf Qūdum/Taḥiyyah

BACKGROUND

'Ṭawāf' is a term that refers to walking around the Ka'bah and constitutes a form of worship, just like prayer. The same way that prayer consists of a number

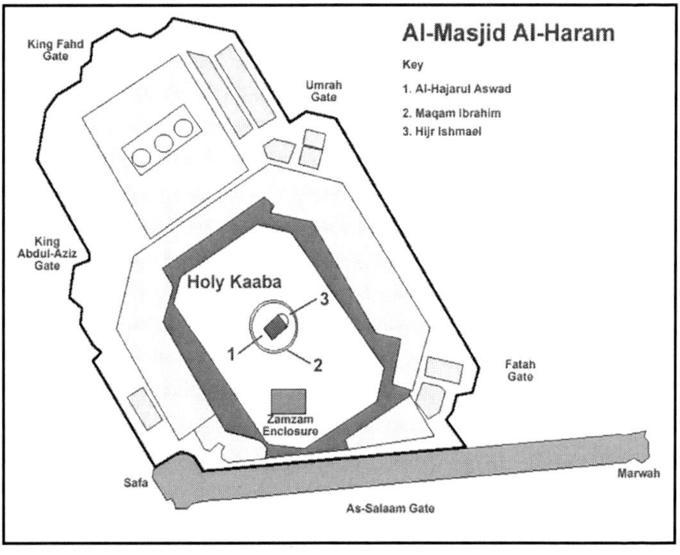

Figure 10: Map of the Sacred Mosque [al-Masjid al-Ḥarām]

of units, there are seven circuits to be made during ṭawāf. Circling the building signifies that Allāh is the center point of your life, since the Kaʿbah remains at the center of your movement.

PREREQUISITES

Ṭawāf is similar to prayer and therefore has the following prerequisites:

- Be in a state of purity by performing wuḍū or taking a bath [if needed]
- Make sure your clothes and body are free of impurities. This is highly recommended but will not invalidate the ṭawāf if violated.
- Make sure your body is covered properly. A male must cover what is between the navel and knees[11] while a woman must cover her entire body except the face, hands, and feet. If a small area is uncovered during ṭawāf, it should be re-covered when detected. However, if a large area is uncovered, the ṭawāf must be restarted.

Similar to prayer, anyone in need of a bath [ghusl] or women who are menstruating or in lochia will not perform ṭawāf.

PURPOSE OF ṬAWĀF QUDŪM/TAḤIYYAH

The ṭawāf qudūm/taḥiyyah is the first act of worship upon visiting the Kaʿbah [hence the meaning qudūm: arrival,

11 Whether or not the knees and navel must be covered is a matter of dispute between Muslim scholars. If it is easy to do so it is always better to cover them.

taḥiyyah: greeting]. If a woman's period ends before she leaves Makkah for Minā on the 8th of Dhul Ḥijjah then she should perform the ṭawāf qudūm/taḥiyyah, otherwise she will skip it since it is not a requirement of Ḥajj.

HOW TO PERFORM ṬAWĀF

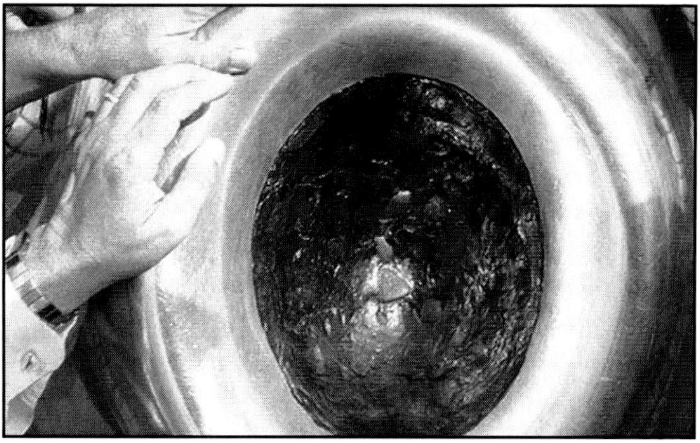

The Black Stone [al-Ḥajar al-Aswad]

The Black Stone [al-Ḥajar al-Aswad] is a marker that is built into one corner of the Kaʿbah and signifies where the ṭawāf begins. It was placed there by Prophet Ibrāhīm when he was constructing the building. It is special because he was not able to find a stone to use as a marker so Allāh sent him this stone to use. The original stone has since been damaged and broken into pieces, and was even stolen for twenty two years by the Qarmatians [from 317-339 A.H.]. Now, the remaining pieces have been combined together in a larger structure.

The Yemeni Corner [Rukn Yamānī]

> *The Yemeni Corner [Rukn Yamānī] is the corner of the Kaʿbah towards Yemen in the south. The Prophet used to touch this corner whenever he walked around it. The reason he did so is because during his time, this section was preserved from the original Kaʿbah, whereas most of the building had been rebuilt.*

After arriving at the Kaʿbah, stop reciting the Response Slogan [talbiyah] and prepare to start the ṭawāf of the Kaʿbah.

- [Men] Adjust your iḥrām clothing so your right shoulder is uncovered [called 'iḍṭibāʿ'] and the other end of the top garment is worn over the left shoulder. It is only to be done during the first ṭawāf upon entering Makkah during a journey. The Prophet Muhammad did this when he visited the Kaʿbah after having migrated to Madīnah because there was a rumor that the Muslims had become weak due to the illnesses in Madīnah at the time. He wanted to show the Arab pagans that the Muslims were still strong and hence this tradition continues until today, even though the original cause does not exist anymore.

- Stand parallel to the Black Stone [al-ḥajar al-aswad], which is the marker for starting the ṭawāf. It is rare for anyone to get close enough to the Black Stone to kiss or touch it for ṭawāf due to crowding nowadays.
  - ✧ Face the Kaʿbah and either kiss the Black Stone [if you can get close enough], touch it [if possible], or gesture towards it with your right hand. Say 'Allāhu Akbar' ['God is the greatest'] while doing this and the ṭawāf will begin. This is similar to raising your hands when beginning prayer.
- Walk around the Ka'bah in a counter-clockwise motion
- It is recommended [if possible] that men increase their speed during the first three rounds [called 'ramal']. This is a symbolic military-like jog in order to show strength, and was done by the Prophet Muhammad for the same reason he uncovered his right shoulder. It is only to be done during the first ṭawāf upon entering Makkah during a journey.
- While circling the Kaʿbah, supplicate to Allah [duʿā'], remember Him [dhikr] and recite Qur'ān. There is nothing specified to be said while making ṭawāf [with one following exception], so see the appendix on 'Suggested Supplications and Remembrances' for recommendations.
- When you are parallel to the Yemeni Corner [Rukn Yamanī] it is recommended to recite the following at least once:

رَبَّنَا آتِنَا فِي الدُّنْيَا حَسَنَةً وَفِي الْآخِرَةِ حَسَنَةً وَقِنَا عَذَابَ النَّارِ

rabbanā ātinā fid-dunyā ḥasanah, wa fil-ākhirati ḥasanah, wa qinā ʿadhāban-nār

Our Lord, give us good in this life, in the next life, and save us from the punishment of the Fire

- Finishing a circuit and arriving parallel to the black stone will count as one round.
- Start the next round in precisely the same way, making sure to keep track how many rounds you have completed.
- Complete a total of seven rounds, ending up parallel to the Black Stone.
- This concludes the ṭawāf. Men should re-cover their right shoulder if this was their first ṭawāf during this journey.

Tips

- When it is very crowded, each round can take about half an hour to complete, so be mentally and physically prepared for that.
- Use a counting device to keep track of how many rounds you have performed.
- Try to make ṭawāf far enough from the Kaʿbah where it is not too crowded in order to avoid injury to yourself or others. If it is too crowded on the ground floor, you may perform it on an upper level.
- Don't try to get near the Black Stone during Ḥajj time since you will either harm yourself or someone else due to overcrowding. There is no sense to do something that is prohibited [harming others/yourself]

in order to achieve something that is only a minor recommendation.

- Forgive people who accidentally/ignorantly push you. It may be annoying, but remind yourself that you are there to worship Allāh, not to stress over the problems in the global Muslim community.

Questions

- Should the prayer for greeting the mosque be performed [ṭaḥiyyatul masjid] in the Sacred Mosque?

  If you immediately begin to perform ṭawāf then no, because performing ṭawāf substitutes for prayer in that regard.

- If I get tired during ṭawāf, can I take a break?

  Yes, that is allowed and you should continue from where you left off.

- Is it allowed to talk to other people or use a cell phone?

  Technically, yes, but the primary purpose of the ṭawāf is to worship Allāh, so only do so when needed.

- If I lose my wuḍū' while performing ṭawāf, what should I do?

  You should leave, perform wuḍū', and then continue from where you left off.

- How can I speed up my pace ['ramal'] during the first three rounds of ṭawāf if it is crowded?

  If it is crowded, you will not be able to do this since other people will be walking slowly, therefore, try to symbolize the jog as much as possible whenever you find an opening or just move your arms to symbolize a power walk.

- If I don't remember how many rounds I have performed, what do I do?

  If you are in doubt about how many rounds you performed, assume the lowest number you think it might be and continue from there. For example, if you don't remember whether you were on round three, four, or five, assume you are on round three.

- Should I supplicate, remember Allāh, and recite Qur'ān out loud during ṭawāf?

  You have the option to either say these things quietly or loud enough so you can hear yourself, but you should not raise your voice so much that it disturbs people around you.

- Is it recommended to gesture a flying kiss towards the Black Stone in case you cannot get near it?

  No, the Companions of the Prophet gestured with their hand towards it if they couldn't get close enough and that is what should be followed.

- Can someone wear sandals or shoes during ṭawāf?

  When men are performing ṭawāf in the state of iḥrām, they will not be allowed to cover their feet. However, women may technically wear socks or shoes. Also, outside of ṭawāf qudūm/taḥiyyah, men will not be in a state of iḥrām when performing ṭawāf and may thus also wear socks or shoes. However, it is important to not make the area dirty, so only wear shoes that are very clean.

- If someone needs to stop performing ṭawāf due to congregational prayer, what should they do?

  They should stop, pray, and then continue their ṭawāf from where they were.

AFTER ṬAWĀF

After ṭawāf, pray two units, preferably behind the Station of Ibrāhīm [Maqām Ibrāhīm]. This is a stone that Prophet Ibrāhīm used to stand on while building the Kaʿbah. It used to be directly next to the Kaʿbah but was moved back a little bit so that people would not run into it when performing ṭawāf. It is said that his footprints were left on the stone.

The Station of Abraham [Maqām Ibrāhīm]

Remember to always face the Kaʿbah when praying. It is not necessary to pray directly behind the Station of Ibrahīm, so you can be in line with it from a distance. If it is very crowded and inconvenient to do so, you may pray these two recommended units anywhere in the Sacred Mosque. It is also recommended to recite sūrah al-kāfirūn [109] in the first unit and sūrah al-ikhlāṣ [112] in the second.

Tips

Don't try to pray directly behind the Station of Ibrāhīm during Ḥajj time since you may harm yourself or someone else due to overcrowding

Walking [Sa'y] between Ṣafā and Marwah

BACKGROUND

When Prophet Ibrāhīm [Abraham] left his wife Ḥājar [Hagar] and son Ismā'īl [Ishamel] in the barren valley of Makkah, they soon ran out of food. She ascended a nearby hill called Ṣafā and searched for help, but no one was to be found. She then walked to another hill across the way called Marwah. She climbed it, looking for help, but again, no one was to be found. She kept pacing gift from Allāh because she put her trust in Allāh. back and forth, between the two hills, seven times, until

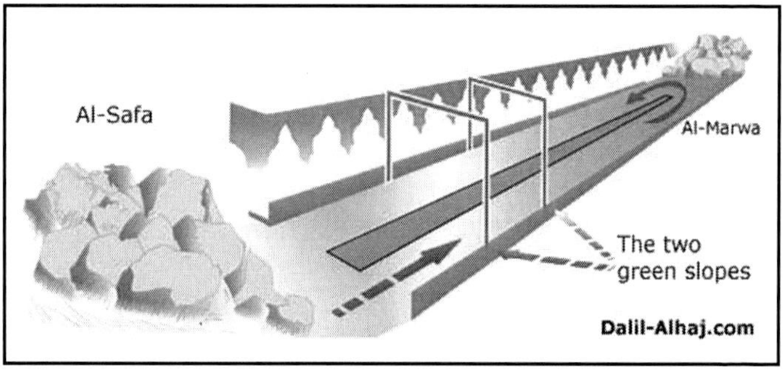

Diagram of Ṣafā and Marwah

she noticed that a well had suddenly sprung up. This is the well of Zamzam and was a

In order to commemorate her test, Muslims are taught to relive her circumstances by walking back and forth between these two hills. This act is known as saʿy, which means walking swiftly.

The Hallway between Ṣafā and Marwah

PREREQUISITES

There are no required prerequisites for saʿy, although it is recommended to be in a state of wuḍūʾ. Women who are in their menstrual or lochia period are recommended to only perform saʿy if they just performed ṭawāf and then their period began, so that both acts are performed back-to-back.

If you chose to perform Ḥajj only [ifrād] or combine Ḥajj and ʿUmrah together [qirān], you are not required to perform this walk [saʿy] right now, but you may if you wish. However, if you are merging ʿUmrah into Ḥajj [tamattuʿ] then you must perform it now.

HOW TO WALK [*Saʿy*] BETWEEN ṢAFĀ AND MARWAH

- Go to Ṣafā hill
- Slightly ascend Ṣafā, face the Kaʿbah, and say 'Allāhu Akbar' ['God is the greatest']. There is no need to climb all the way to the top of the hill.
- Raise your hands and supplicate to Allāh.
- Walk from Ṣafā to Marwah while supplicating to Allāh [duʿā'], remembering Him [dhikr] and reciting Qur'ān. There is nothing specified to be said while walking, so see the appendix on 'Suggested Supplications and Remembrances' for recommendations.
- It is recommended to run or jog between the two green columns that are marked in the walking area. Ḥājar had left her son Ismāʿīl on the ground to make her mission to find help easier. When she was in the valley between the two hills, she was not able to see her son, so she ran through the area where he was not visible, and then continued walking at a normal pace when she was able to see him again. It is commendable to imitate her act.
- Ascend Marwah, face the Kaʿbah, and supplicate to Allāh as before.
- This walk between Ṣafā and Marwah will count as one trip.

- Descend Marwah and walk back to Ṣafā, doing the same thing as before. This will complete your second trip.
- Complete seven trips, ending up at Marwah. Supplicate to Allāh as before. The walking [saʿy] is complete.

TIPS

The two hills of Ṣafā and Marwah are about 980 feet apart, so seven trips will equal about 1.3 miles [2.1 kilometers] of distance. Be physically and mentally prepared for that.

Be cautious when ascending and descending the hills, as it can be dangerous when there is a crowd.

There is wheelchair access for those who have major difficulty walking. Also, watch out for wheelchairs hitting you from behind, as it can be very painful.

If the ground floor is too crowded with people, you can perform the walking [saʿy] from the upper levels as well, since it is a symbolic action.

QUESTIONS

- Should the right shoulder be uncovered when walking between Ṣafā and Marwah?

  No, that is only for ṭawāf.

- If I am very tired after performing ṭawāf, can I leave and rest before performing the walking [saʿy]?

  Yes, there would be no harm in that.

- If I get tired during the walking [saʿy], can I take a break?

Yes, that is allowed and you will continue from where you left off.

- If you need to stop performing the walking [saʿy] due to congregational prayer, what should you do?

  You should stop, pray, and then continue from where you were.

- Is it allowed to talk to other people or use a cell phone?

  Technically, yes, but the primary purpose is to worship Allāh, so only do that if needed.

Release from Iḥrām

If you chose to merge ʿUmrah into Ḥajj [tamattuʿ], you will now be released from the state of iḥrām by shaving/trimming your hair. If you chose to combine ʿUmrah and Ḥajj [qirān] or to perform Ḥajj only [ifrād], you will skip this step and remain in the state of iḥrām until later.

Men must now shave or trim their hair in order to be released from iḥrām, which is similar to concluding the prayer with saying salām. Shaving the hair off is normally preferred, but you may also shorten your hair instead by trimming at least about a fingertip length from all over the head. If you were to shave your head and it would not likely grow back much until the 8th of Dhul Ḥijjah, it is better to trim instead of shaving, since you will do this again in a few days. Women must not shave their head, but they must shorten their hair by trimming it.

The ʿUmrah is now complete and you are released from the state of iḥrām, so the restrictions of iḥrām no longer apply. You may now change your clothes, apply fragrance, etc.

TIPS

Do not cut your hair inside the mosque because it will dirty the area.

There are barbers nearby right outside when you leave Marwah.

QUESTIONS

- Can I cut my own hair or someone else's hair while I am still in the state of iḥrām?

  Yes, that is allowed.

- Is it fine to just cut a few strands of hair from different places of the head?

  No, hair should be trimmed evenly throughout the head, depending on the style of the haircut. At minimum, at least twenty-five percent of the hair on the head must be cut in some fashion.

Day One—8th of Dhul Ḥijjah

OVERVIEW

You will travel to Minā in the state of iḥrām and spend the whole day and night there.

ENTER THE STATE OF IḤRĀM

If you chose to combine ʿUmrah and Ḥajj [qirān] or to perform Ḥajj only [ifrād], you will already be in the state of iḥrām so you can skip this step.

Sometime after sunrise, enter into the state of iḥrām [refer back to the section on 'Entering the State of Iḥrām'].

Tips

You will be in the state of iḥrām for about forty eight hours so be mentally prepared.

STAYING AT MINĀ

Background

Minā is a region in Makkah where Prophet Ibrāhīm went to fulfill Allāh's command to sacrifice his son Ismāʿīl. There is also a mosque called Masjid al-Khayf near the markers where Prophet Muhammad prayed with his Companions.

TRAVEL TO MINĀ

While in the state of iḥrām, travel to Minā either by walking or by taking transportation. It is recommended to arrive there before high-noon.

Spend the entire day at Minā while shortening your four unit prayers to two units. This shortening will occur at Minā throughout the Ḥajj and is not limited to this day only. It is recommended to pray the witr prayer after ʿishā', but other recommended prayers may be skipped.

Tips

Ensure you are within the proper boundaries of Minā. There are signposts indicating the borders.

It may take up to five hours or more to reach Minā due to traffic congestion, so be mentally and physically prepared.

Day Two—9th of Dhul Ḥijjah

OVERVIEW

You will leave Minā in the morning and stay at ʿArafāt until sunset. You will then travel to Muzdalifah and spend the night there.

ATTENDING ʿARAFĀT

Background

The plain of ʿArafāt is outside of Makkah. This is the area where Prophet Muhammad delivered his famous Farewell Sermon in front of over a hundred thousand believers. There is now a mosque at this location called Masjid an-Namirah. There is also a mountain nicknamed the Mountain of Mercy [Jabal ar-Raḥmah] because the mercy of Allāh descends on the people praying and asking for forgiveness in this entire area of ʿArafāt.

THE PLAIN OF ʿARAFĀT

After praying fajr at Minā, leave for ʿArafāt by walking or by taking transportation. Try to arrive by ẓuhr time. You must arrive before sunset and stay at least a few moments after sunset.

At ʿArafah, shorten [to two units] and combine ẓuhr and ʿasr prayers by praying them back-to-back during the normal timing for ẓuhr. If you arrive late, then shorten and combine them during ʿasr time. The purpose of combining these prayers is so that you can focus entirely on supplicating to Allāh while you are at ʿArafāt. Your time here is considered to be the most important part of Ḥajj.

At ʿArafāt you should remember Allāh [dhikr] and supplicate to Him [duʿā']. It is especially recommended to ask for forgiveness for all your sins here. Also, remember to say the Response Slogan [talbiyah] every once in a while. It is preferable to stand, raise your hands, and face the qiblah [the direction of the Kaʿbah] when supplicating. It is fine to lower your hands or sit when you need a break.

Continue this way until sunset. There is no need to be near or on the Mountain of Mercy [Jabal ar-Raḥmah].

Tips

It may take up to ten hours or more to reach ʿArafāt due to traffic congestion, so be mentally and physically prepared.

Make sure to depart from Minā early because if you fail to arrive in ʿArafāt before the following day, you might invalidate the entire Ḥajj.

Make sure to not waste time socializing since this is the most important part of Ḥajj and where supplications are most-answered.

STAYING IN MUZDALIFAH

Background

Muzdalifah is a region where the Prophet Muhammad stopped to rest on his way back from ʿArafah to Minā.

REST AT MUZDALIFAH

Leave ʿArafāt after sunset, without praying maghrib, and travel to Muzdalifah. Once you arrive, pray maghrib and ʿishā' [shortened from four to two units] combined during the time for ʿishā'. If you arrive early, delay your prayers until the time for ʿishā' comes in, but if your arrival will be delayed past midnight, then combine the prayers wherever you may be.

If convenient, collect seven or forty-nine small pebbles [around the size of a chickpea] from Muzdalifah. You will use these pebbles at Minā and will learn later why this many are needed. Muzdalifah has a lot of pebbles, but if you prefer, you can collect them from any other location that is convenient.

Find a place to sleep and get some rest. This is not the time for extra prayers since the following day will be very busy and you will need your energy.

Questions

- If someone finds great difficulty in staying at Muzdalifah, can they go straight back to Minā?

  People who are old, weak, or ill may leave Muzdalifah early after staying briefly at night. If someone is taking care of one of these excused people, they may also leave with them. However, people who are in good health are not allowed to take this exception.

Day Three—10th of Dhul Ḥijjah

OVERVIEW

You will leave Muzdalifah and return to Minā. There, you will throw seven pebbles, offer an animal sacrifice, and shave your head. Many people will also go to the Kaʿbah and perform a ṭawāf on this day.

LEAVING MUZDALIFAH

Pray fajr at Muzdalifah. After fajr, remember Allāh and supplicate to Him until sunrise.

Travel back to Minā after sunrise.

Questions

- Is it recommended to wash the pebbles you collect so they are clean?

  There is no need to do that unless you suspect that they may have some impurities on them.

- What type of pebbles should be picked up?

Any pebble that is from the makeup of the earth's surface will suffice.

FIRST STONING AT MINĀ

Background

When Prophet Ibrāhīm was on his way to sacrifice his son, as commanded by Allah, Satan [Shayṭān] tried to tempt him to disobey the order. Satan appeared to him three times suggesting that he abandon the idea, but each time Prophet Ibrāhīm picked up some stones and threw them at him, signifying his rejection of Satan and obedience to Allah. There is an area in Minā which has three markers to indicate the locations where this occurred, and Muslims commemorate the piety of Prophet Ibrāhīm by throwing stones at the same area, signifying that they also reject Satan and his temptations.

Stoning Marker [Jamrah] c. 1990 C.E.

The Three Stoning Markers [Jamarāt] c. 2014 C.E.

Upon your return to Minā, you will stone only one of the three markers. Go to the large Stoning Marker [al-Jamrah al-Kubrā], which is the one closest to the direction of the Kaʿbah. All three markers have recently been renovated and are large walls. It is recommended to perform stoning sometime between sunrise and noon, however, it is fine to delay it until later in the day, as long as the stoning is done before sunset. If there is a massive crowd or there is some other excuse, then it is fine to perform it in the night, as long as it is before dawn [this is disliked without a legitimate excuse].

Stop reciting the Response Slogan [talbiyah] once you arrive near the Stoning Marker. Throw seven pebbles at the wall with your right hand. Say 'Allāhu Akbar' before throwing each one, and throw them consecutively. There is no need to throw very hard since this is a symbolic gesture. People who are weak or ill may give their pebbles to someone else to throw on their behalf.

Tips

If it is crowded, you may throw from the upper levels

Be careful not to miss when throwing because you might hit someone in the head

Questions

- If someone throws two pebbles at once, will it count as one or two?

  It will count as one throw and they will have to throw an extra pebble.

- Can the weak and ill who left Muzdalifah early throw their pebbles before sunrise to avoid the crowds?

  No, because there is no urgent need to do so. It is better for them to wait until the evening.

SACRIFICING AN ANIMAL

If you chose to merge ʿUmrah into Ḥajj [tamattuʿ] or combine ʿUmrah and Ḥajj [qirān], you must offer an animal sacrifice as a way of thanking Allāh for allowing you to combine two acts of worship together. If you performed Ḥajj only [ifrād] then you are not required to do so.

The animal offered must be one goat, sheep, or lamb. Alternatively, seven people can share in sacrificing one cow or camel, since they are much larger animals. After sacrificing the animal, you may eat up to one-third of the meat, offer up to one-third as a gift to friends and family, and distribute the rest to the poor. However, due to the vast number of people attending Ḥajj, a slaughtering company handles the sacrifice for most people who pay them to do so. This meat is packaged and distributed to people in need and therefore, all the meat is given in charity.

SHAVING HEAD

Once the sacrifice is complete you will now shave/trim your hair. Remember that shaving the hair is normally preferred for men. At this point, all restrictions of iḥrām are lifted except intercourse. You may now change your clothes and apply some fragrance.

Questions

- How can I know when my animal has been sacrificed? If the company I paid slaughters it after several days, must I remain in the state of iḥrām?

  Since there is no way to verify if the slaughter has been completed, it should be assumed that the slaughter was performed on the morning of the 10th of Dhul Ḥijjah, since that is when they begin slaughtering animals. There are millions of animals being slaughtered and it would be very difficult to inform every person when their animal was slaughtered. Therefore, you can safely assume an animal has been slaughtered on your behalf.

ṬAWĀF IFĀḌAH/ZIYĀRAH

Go to Makkah to perform a ṭawāf of the Kaʿbah. This ṭawāf may be performed anytime from fajr on the 10th of Dhul Ḥijjah until the 13th of Dhul Ḥijjah. Due to massive crowding, it might even be recommended to delay it a day or two.

Perform ṭawāf, like before, but in your normal clothes.

Tips

It is recommended to perform this ṭawāf either at night, or a day or two later so that there is less crowding.

Questions

- How can a menstruating woman or one with lochia perform this ṭawāf, since it is a very important part of Ḥajj?

  If a woman has her period during this time, she must wait in Makkah until it ends and then perform ṭawāf ifāḍah/ziyārah. However, if her period does not end before she must leave Makkah [due to her group traveling, not being able to change her ticket, etc.], it is fine for her to perform this ṭawāf right before leaving Makkah, even during her period, as an exception to the rule.

WALKING [*Saʿy*] BETWEEN ṢAFĀ AND MARWAH

After ṭawāf, perform the walk [saʿy] between Ṣafā and Marwah as before. Those who chose to perform Ḥajj only [ifrād] or ʿUmrah and Ḥajj combined [qirān] are exempted from this if they already performed this previously with the ṭawāf qudūm.

Once this is done, you are now completely released from the state of iḥrām and intercourse is allowed as well.

STAYING AT MINĀ

Return to Minā. Spend the night there, making sure to be in Minā at least from midnight to sunrise.

Day Four—11th of Dhul Ḥijjah

STONING THE THREE MARKERS [*Jamarāt*]

If you don't already have them, collect twenty one pebbles from anywhere. Head towards the three Stoning Markers [jamarāt] between ẓuhr and sunset. It is allowed to delay this until fajr of the next day if needed.

Starting with the small Stoning Marker [al-jamrah aṣ-ṣughrā], throw seven pebbles. Move back to a less crowded area, face the direction of prayer [qiblah], and supplicate [du'ā'] to Allāh.

Then proceed to the medium Stoning Marker [al-jamrah al-wuṣṭā] and do the same.

Finally, proceed to the large Stoning Marker [al-jamrah al-kubrā] and do the same, but do not supplicate this time.

STAYING AT MINĀ

Spend the night at Minā, making sure to be there at least from midnight to sunrise.

Day Five—12th of Dhul Ḥijjah

Repeat the stoning at all three markers as you did the previous day. Before sunset, decide whether you want to remain in Minā another day or return to Makkah. If you plan on leaving, which is optional, you must do so before maghrib, otherwise you are required to spend another day in Minā.

Day Six [Optional]—13th of Dhul Ḥijjah

If you chose to remain in Minā, repeat the stoning at all three markers as you did the previous day. Then return to Makkah.

FAREWELL ṬAWĀF [*Wadāʿ/Ṣadr*]

Many people choose to stay in Makkah for a while before returning back home. You may stay for as long as you like, but right before you leave Makkah, you must perform a ṭawāf, similar to the ṭawāf ifāḍah/ziyārah since you will be in your normal clothes. This should be the last thing you do, within your reasonable control, before leaving the city.

This completes your Ḥajj journey. Make the intention to change your life and never disobey Allāh again.

QUESTIONS

- If you are with a group and some people are delayed after you have performed your final ṭawāf, do you need to perform it again?

No, since determining the timing of what other people might do is beyond your control. You may do other things while waiting for your group such as shopping, eating, etc.

- Is it required to check out of your hotel before performing the final ṭawāf?

  If there is difficulty in doing so, because you have no place to keep your luggage for example, then it is fine to check out afterwards.

- What should a woman do during her period if she is planning on leaving Makkah?

  Women in their period are excused from performing this final ṭawāf, so they can skip it.

- Is it allowed to delay the ṭawāf ifāḍah/ziyārah until just before you leave Makkah, so you can consider this your farewell ṭawāf as well?

  Technically this is allowed but disliked, since it is a stratagem to do less than what was originally required.

- If I leave Makkah for Madīnah and then plan to return soon, should a farewell ṭawāf be performed?

  No, since you are not leaving for your home. This is similar to a person traveling to the outskirts of Makkah for some reason, and then returning back.

Mistakes and Penalties

You might make a mistake in some part of Ḥajj for one reason or another. Some mistakes may invalidate the entire Ḥajj, others require sacrificing an animal or giving charity as a penalty, and yet others do not affect the validity of the Ḥajj. An animal sacrifice consists of slaughtering a sheep, goat, or lamb in Makkah while giving charity entails distributing at least six meals to the poor.

These are among the common mistakes that are made, along with explanations of what must be done:

- Violating iḥrām regulations: whether intentionally, with an excuse, or accidentally
  - ✧ If you had the intention to go to Makkah and crossed a mīqāt boundary without assuming iḥrām, then:
    - You should return back to the mīqāt boundary and assume iḥrām.
    - If you do not return back, assume iḥrām from wherever you are, and you must offer a penalty sacrifice.
  - ✧ If you apply any scent to your body or clothes

- Where it affects one whole area of the body like the hand or the head, you must offer a penalty sacrifice.
- If you applied such a small amount that it affects less than that area, you must give charity.

✧ If you cover your head or face
- For an entire day, you must offer a penalty sacrifice.
    - If you covered for less than that time, you must give charity.
- Covering only a small portion of the head or face will require giving charity.

✧ If you shave or trim
- A large area like a fourth of your head, one underarm, etc., you must offer a penalty sacrifice.
    - If you shaved or trimmed less than that, you must give charity.

✧ If you cut your nails
- You must offer a penalty sacrifice.
    - If you cut less than five nails, you must give charity for each nail cut.

✧ If you have intercourse
- Prior to staying at ʿArafah, you must offer a penalty sacrifice and your Ḥajj will be invalid, although you must complete this one as well. You must perform another Ḥajj to make up for this one.
    - If after staying at ʿArafah, both partners must each offer a penalty sacrifice.

- Making a mistake at ʿArafāt:

✧ If you do not stay at ʿArafāt on the 9th of Dhul Ḥijjah, your Ḥajj will be invalid, you must offer a penalty sacrifice, and perform Ḥajj again.

- ✧ If you leave ʿArafāt before sunset, you must offer a penalty sacrifice.
- ✧ If you arrive in ʿArafāt after sunset but before fajr of the following day, you must offer a penalty sacrifice.

- Making a mistake at Muzdalifah:
    - ✧ If you leave Muzdalifah before fajr without an excuse, you must offer a penalty sacrifice.
    - ✧ Those who have an excuse such as the weak and ill may leave Muzdalifah after midnight, without any penalty.

- Mistakes on the 10th of Dhul Ḥijjah:
    - ✧ If you delay the first throwing of pebbles beyond fajr time [since it would be the following day], you must offer a penalty sacrifice. It must still be performed as soon as possible.
    - ✧ If you do not perform the First Throwing, shaving the head, and sacrificing an animal in that specific order, you must offer a penalty sacrifice. However, if you perform the Ṭawāf Ziyārah prior to any of these, it is disliked but no penalty sacrifice is needed.

- Mistakes at Mina:
    - ✧ If you skip throwing twenty one pebbles on either the 11th or the 12th, then you must make it up before sunset of the 13th day and must offer a penalty sacrifice for delaying it.
    - ✧ If you threw less than seven pebbles at any Stoning Marker
        - If you threw four or more, it counts as most, and you will offer charity for each pebble missed

  - If you threw less than four, it will not count and you must repeat the stoning

- Mistakes in Ṭawāf:
  - ✧ If you perform ṭawāf without wuḍū', you must offer a penalty sacrifice, unless you redo the ṭawāf again with wuḍū'.
  - ✧ If you get transport assistance (such as a wheelchair) while you have the capability of walking, you must offer a penalty sacrifice.
  - ✧ If you uncover more than a fourth of a body part that must be covered during ṭawāf, you must offer a penalty sacrifice.
  - ✧ If you skip the two units of prayer after the ṭawāf, you must offer a penalty sacrifice.
  - ✧ If you skip performing the Ṭawāf Ziyārah/Ifāḍah entirely, your Ḥajj will not count, and you must offer a penalty sacrifice as well.
  - ✧ If you delay the Ṭawāf Ziyārah/Ifāḍah past sunset of the 13th of Dhul Ḥijjah then you must offer a penalty sacrifice.
  - ✧ If you skip the Farewell Ṭawāf, you must offer a penalty sacrifice, except for women during their period.

- Mistakes in Walking [Saʿy] between Ṣafā and Marwah
  - ✧ If you skip the saʿy, you must offer a penalty sacrifice.

If you are prevented from completing Ḥajj due to an illness or other reason, you must offer a penalty sacrifice and then be released from iḥrām. The obligation of Ḥajj is not lifted and you must perform it again when able.

TIPS

An animal sacrifice costs about US $140 in Makkah. You may purchase a ticket at the local bank and they will perform it for you.

What to do in Makkah

WORSHIP

While ṭawāf is performed during Ḥajj and Umrah, you can perform an optional [nafl] ṭawāf at any time. The Sacred Mosque [al-Masjid al-Ḥarām] is similar to any other mosque with the exception that this is the only place in the world where ṭawāf can be performed, so it is recommended to perform as many as possible. Ṭawāf can be done at any time of the day and is similar to prayers. It is necessary to have wuḍū' but you can wear any clothes, as long as they are clean, just like the other prayers. There is no need to be in the state of iḥrām when performing optional [nafl] ṭawāfs.

Each prayer in the Sacred Mosque is 100,000 times superior to a prayer in any other mosque. Therefore, try to perform as many prayers in the mosque as possible.

HISTORICAL SITES

There are many historical sites worth visiting in the city of Makkah as well. Research in order to learn more about them.

QUESTIONS

- If there is a prayer area in my hotel where the prayer from the Sacred Mosque is being broadcast live, can I pray there and count it as being with the congregation? What if I can see the Ka'bah from this room, or from my hotel room, and I can hear the imam [leader of the prayer], will it count as if I was praying with the people in the Sacred Mosque?

  In order for a person to be considered as part of a congregational prayer, there must be no unnecessary gap between the imām and the followers. A necessary gap would consist of buildings, large objects, or other obstructions that cannot be moved easily. You should not be lazy and you must leave your hotel in order to fill in the gaps between the rows of worshippers, as much as possible.

Visiting Madīnah

The city of the Prophet [Madīnat un-Nabī], formerly known as Yathrib, is 210 miles north of Makkah. It is a fertile area with a population of about 1.3 million people [2006]. The mosque of the Prophet [Masjid an-Nabī] located here is the second most important site in Islām and it is recommended to visit it, if you are able.

There is immense historical value in visiting the city as well since it is where the Qur'ān was revealed for ten years. It is also where the Prophet and most of his Companions lived.

THE PROPHET'S MOSQUE

When visiting the mosque of the Prophet, it is recommended to offer two units of prayer as a greeting of the mosque. The original area of the mosque built by the Prophet is known as the rawḍah area and is recognized by carpeting of a different color. The Prophet said about this area: "Between my house and my pulpit is a garden [rawḍah] of Paradise."[12] Therefore, it is recommended to

12 Bukhārī and Muslim

try to pray at least once in this area, if it is not too crowded. The Prophet said, "Any prayer in my mosque is better than one thousand prayers in any other mosque, except for the Sacred Mosque [in Makkah]."[13] Therefore, it is recommended to pray in this mosque as much as possible when in Madīnah.

The Prophet was buried in his house, which was adjacent to the mosque. After the necessary expansion of the mosque by Walīd I [d. 715], his grave was included in the structure of the mosque itself. It is recommended to pass by the Prophet's grave and greet him by saying "as-salāmu ʿalaykum yā rasūl Allāh" ["peace be upon you, Messenger of Allāh"]. Buried next to him are Abū Bakr and ʿUmar and it is recommended to greet them as well. It is also recommended to supplicate to Allāh while passing by, but make sure to face the direction of prayer [qiblah] and only direct your supplication towards Allāh.

TIPS

Remember not to exaggerate in your love of the Prophet by wailing loudly while passing by his grave or directing your supplications to him instead of Allah.

HISTORICAL SITES

There are many historical sites worth visiting in the city of Madīnah as well. Research in order to learn more about them.

13 Tirmidhī

QUESTIONS

- Is it recommended to pray a certain number of prayers in Madīnah?

  No. The commonly held view that one should pray forty prayers here is based on weak evidence.

- Is it disrespectful to turn your back to the Prophet's grave?

  No, there is no basis for that notion.

Appendix: The Standard Ḥajj Schedule

DAY	ACTIONS
Before Makkah	*Assume Iḥrām*
Arriving in Makkah	*Ṭawāf & Sa'y**
8th of Dhul Ḥijjah	*Stay at Minā*
9th of Dhul Ḥijjah	*Stay at 'Arafah* *Sleep in Muzdalifah*
10th of Dhul Ḥijjah	*Stone the large Marker at Minā* *Offer a sacrifice* *Shave head* *Exit Iḥrām [mostly]* *Visitation Ṭawāf**
11th of Dhul Ḥijjah	*Stone the three Markers at Minā*
12th of Dhul Ḥijjah	*Stone the three Markers at Minā*
13th of Dhul Ḥijjah [Optional]	*Stone the three Markers at Minā**
Before Leaving Makkah	*Farewell Ṭawāf*

Appendix: Selected Supplications [du'ā'] and Remembrances [dhikr]

Supplication is an essential practice in the life of a Muslim. Be persistent in asking and never lose hope. Know that Allāh answers all prayers in some way, shape, or form.

All supplications outside of prayer may be made in any language. The best supplication is what is said with humility and sincerity, rather than merely parroting a memorized formula with little concentration. It is recommended to always raise your hands like a beggar when asking Allāh for something in order to exhibit more humility, except during ṭawāf, prayer, or saʿy since raising your hands would distract from the motions of these acts.

Here are some recommended supplications and remembrances:

> *"Our Lord! Accept (this service) from us. Surely You are the All-Hearing, the All-Knowing.*[14]

---

14 Qur'an 2:127

"Our Lord, grant us in the world what is good, and in the Hereafter what is good, and protect us from the punishment of the Fire."[15]

"Our Lord, take us not to task if we forget or make mistakes. Our Lord, lay not on us a burden such as You laid on those gone before us. Our Lord, impose not on us what we do not have the power to bear. Overlook our faults, forgive us, and have mercy on us. You are our Guardian and Owner [to Whom We entrust our affairs] so help us and grant us victory against the disbelieving people."[16]

"Our Lord, do not let our hearts swerve after You have guided us, and bestow upon us mercy from Your Presence. Surely You are the All-Bestowing."[17]

"Our Lord, we do indeed believe, so forgive us our sins and guard us against the punishment of the Fire."[18]

"Our Lord! We believe in what You have sent down, and we follow the Messenger, so write us down among the witnesses."[19]

"Our Lord! Forgive us our sins and any major sin we may have done in our actions, and set our feet firm, and help us to victory over the disbelieving people!"[20]

15 Qur'an 2:201

16 Qur'an 2:286

17 Qur'an 3:8

18 Qur'an 3:16

19 Qur'an 3:53

20 Qur'an 3:147

"Our Lord! We have wronged ourselves, and if You do not forgive us and do not have mercy on us, we will surely be among those who have lost!"[21]

"Glory to Allah, Praise to Allah, there is no god besides Allah, Allah is great."

21 Qur'an 7:23

Appendix: The Funeral Prayer

It is recommended to learn how to perform the funeral prayer since many of them are offered in Makkah and Madīnah regularly.

Appendix: Differences of Opinion

It is important to remember that Muslims scholars have different opinions in certain practices of Islam, and Ḥajj is no exception. For example, prominent Muslim scholars since the time of the Companions of the Prophet have different opinions concerning the following:

- Are there supposed to be two calls to initiate prayer [iqāmah] or one when in Muzdalifah
- Which of the three types of Ḥajj has greater reward: combining Ḥajj and ʿUmrah together [qirān], performing Ḥajj separately [ifrād], or merging ʿUmrah into Ḥajj [tamattuʿ]
- Is it recommended to leave Muzdalifah before or after sunrise

It is from Allah's wisdom and mercy that he allowed scholars to hold differences of opinion. The following incidents demonstrate Islam's stance on differences in understanding what Allah and His Messenger really intended:

- A group of Muslims were on a journey together when, all of a sudden, a piece of rock fell from a mountain and hit one of them in the head. The man was badly injured so he bandaged his wound and they continued on their journey. The next morning, he discovered that he had a wet dream at night and now needed to take a bath before prayer. The man asked his fellow Muslims whether there was any exception to the rule for him since he was injured. They replied in the negative and insisted that he must take a bath and wash his head. When the man removed his bandage and poured water over his head, he fell down and died. After returning from their journey they told the Prophet what had happened. He was furious, and responded, "They killed him! Allah might kill them! If they don't know, why don't they ask? Asking is the cure for ignorance." Then he explained to them that the man didn't have to wash his head because of his injury.[22]
- The Prophet ordered his companions to set out for a military expedition and instructed them, "Do not pray the ʿAsr prayer until you reach Banū Qurayẓah [a village near Madīnah]." A group of them were delayed on the way and the time for the ʿAsr prayer was almost finished. Some of them decided not to pray until they arrived, taking the Prophet's words literally. Others from the group insisted: "We will pray. The Prophet didn't mean that we should skip the prayer." After they arrived, they informed the Prophet what had happened, and he didn't criticize either of them for what they did.[23]

22 Abū Dāwūd, *al-Sunan*, 1:93, #336.

23 Al-Bukhārī, *al-Ṣaḥīḥ*, 2:15, #946.

These two incidents demonstrate that there is room in Islam for differences of opinion within certain bounds. Sometimes a person may be blatantly wrong in one's opinion, like the Muslims who insisted that the man wash his injured head. Another time, two different opinions may be right at the same time. In the end, there are two criteria that must be applied in order to determine whether an opinion is legitimate [i.e. accepted by Allah] or not: being sincere in attempting to arrive at what Allah and His Messenger intended and having a solid grounding in knowledge to interpret the sources correctly.

People deal with scholarly differences of opinion during Ḥajj in various ways. One extreme is for a person to assume that his own opinion is the only valid one and he thus tries to correct others whenever they do something different. Another equally extreme view is that of passive relativism where a person does not care whether others are making mistakes or not. The first approach fails to take into consideration that there may be two equally valid [i.e. in the sight of Allah] scholarly opinions on an issue while the second approach fails to care that a Muslim is making a mistake in an act of worship.

It is highly recommended for an ordinary Muslim to either follow what is in this book or rely on their Ḥajj leader [who should be trained in Islamic Law]. Then, if you see someone doing something contrary to what you have learned, you should investigate why that person is doing so. If it is determined that they are doing so out of ignorance, then you must correct that person. However, if it is determined that they are doing so because they learned a different opinion from a legitimate Muslim scholar or book[24], then you should not correct them and be content that you have learned something new [i.e. that there is another scholarly opinion on this issue].

24 Defining exactly who is a Muslim scholar is beyond the scope of this book. The general rule is to always give people who have some credentials the benefit of the doubt.

Appendix: Avoiding Difficulties

One principle that applies to all issues in Islamic law is that difficulty necessitates ease. This axiom means that whenever a person faces a very difficult circumstance, there is usually an exception to the rule. For example, one who has difficulty standing for prayer may sit or lie down instead.

Several common exceptions to the rule regarding Ḥajj have already been mentioned in this book. However, it is important to note that when a person, or group, is faced with difficulty when trying to follow the guidance of Islam, there may be an exception to the rule to ease that difficulty. The best course of action is to ask a scholar specialized in the field of Islamic law whether or not an exception may apply. Never attempt to make exceptions yourself unless you are properly trained in the subject. This is because only an expert would know exactly how the exception should be made. For example, a person who is injured might know that they don't have to perform all the actions of prayer, but does it mean that the prayer should be skipped, delayed, or performed in a different way? That question is not something that the untrained individual can figure out on their own.

Also keep in mind that there are certain difficulties associated with Ḥajj that are a result of the changed circumstances of the times in which we live. For example, it is customary for people to travel using modern vehicles rather than riding on animals as was done in the past. This technological evolution, coupled with the massive increase in the number of people performing Ḥajj nowadays, results in traffic jams. It is important to realize that not every recommended act may be performed at its due time because of the modified circumstances. For example, it may be difficult to:

- Arrive at certain locations on time due to heavy traffic on the roads
- Jog during first three rounds around the Kaʿbah due to overcrowding
- Bathe right before entering Makkah since most people will be in a car or on an airplane
- Perform ṭawāf on the 10th of Dhul Ḥijjah because of overcrowding

Such actions are recommended under normal circumstances but there is no need to put yourself, or your group, in difficult to achieve these actions. The status of their recommended nature may have changed due to the modified circumstances people find themselves in today. Remember that Allah knows your inner intentions and that you would have performed every act at its recommended time had the circumstances been normal. It is hoped that you will be rewarded for you intention, since these circumstances were beyond your control.

References

'Abdullāh ibn Maḥmūd al-Mawṣilī, al-ikhtiyār li-ta'līl al-mukhtār.

http://www.daruliftaa.com/

http://en.islamtoday.net/

Made in United States
Cleveland, OH
03 April 2025

15773211R00057